Black Book

Learn Java™ 8
In a Week

A Beginner's Guide to Java Programming

Mahavir DS Rathore

Books by Mahavir DS Rathore

a. Java 8 Exception Handling
b. Java 8 Exception Handling Quiz

Copyright

Learn Java™ 8 in a Week is by Mahavir DS Rathore. While every precaution has been taken in the preparation of this book the author assume No responsibility for errors or omissions, or for damages resulting from the use of the information contained herein.

About the author

I have been programming and teaching Java for last 18 years. This book is an effort to document my knowledge to share with everyone across the world. I am available to do training on Java anywhere in the world. My email id is gurumahaveer@gmail.com.

Who should read the book?

This book is for programmers who already know some programming language and are keen to learn Java.

Software Required

Java 8 (JDK 1.8) and Notepad++ editor.

Acknowledgement

Java is owned by Oracle and trademark is acknowledged.

Dedication

To my Guru Shri Amrite.

Source Code

For source code of this book please send me a mail at gurumahaveer@gmail.com.

Feedback

Please share your feedback which will help me to improve this book.

Table of Content

Chapter 1
What is Java?

Introduction
The current (Latest) version of Java is 8. Java can be classified and defined into two categories.
   a. Software Platform.
   b. Programming Language.

Java as Software Platform
Java platform is a collection of software components which allow development and execution of bytecode based languages. Bytecode is binary code that Java platform interpret. The Java platform is composed of

   a. Compiler – It generate bytecode from source code
   b. Java Virtual Machine – It provide runtime execution environment for bytecode.
   c. Libraries – It contain Java API.
   d. Tools – Various Java Tools.

The Java bytecode has two important characteristics
   a. It is processor independent i.e. the program can run on any processor architecture.
   b. It is Operating System independent i.e. bytecode does not target any Operating System such as Windows or Linux.

The Java platform is available in four flavors based upon device type.
   a. Java Card – It is used in smart cards and small memory devices.
   b. Java ME (Micro Edition) – It is used in Personnel Digital Assistants, Setup Box and printers application.
   c. Java SE (Standard Edition) – It is used in development of desktop, communication and User Interface based applications.
   d. Java EE (Enterprise Edition) – It is used in development of web based, messaging, distributed and enterprise applications.

The Java Platform has support for many languages such as
   a. Java

b. Jython
c. Jruby
d. Scala
e. Groovy
f. Rakudo Perl 6
g. Kotlin

Java as Programming Language

Java is multi paradigm programming language. It is one of the most used programming language for development of various types of software such as desktop, enterprise, web based and mobile applications.

Some of important attributes of Java Language are
a. Statically typed – The type of the variable is known at compile time.
b. Object oriented – Object centered programming.
c. Concurrent – Support for multithreading programming.
d. Reflective – Allows inspection of class, method, interface, fields.

Languages That Influenced Java

Java language falls in 'C' family of language category. It has taken inspiration from many languages including languages which were released after Java. Some of the major languages that have influenced Java are:
a. C++
b. Oberon
c. Ada 83
d. C#
e. Object Pascal

Languages Influenced by Java

As per tiobe index Java is the No.1 Programming language today. Java has influenced many Modern languages such as:
a. C#
b. Clojure
c. Python
d. JavaScript
e. PHP
f. Scala
g. Groovy

Summary

Java is a programming language and a platform. Java platform is divided into 4 parts – SE, ME, EE and Card. Java is multi-paradigm programming language.

Chapter 2
Java Development Kit and Java Runtime Engine

<u>Topics</u>
- ✓ **Introduction**
- ✓ **Java Runtime Engine**
- ✓ **Java Development Kit**
- ✓ **Installing JDK**
- ✓ **Installing Notepad++**
- ✓ **Summary**

Introduction

The minimum environment required for a java program to run is called JRE (Java Runtime Engine). JDK is the minimum environment required for development of Java Applications.

Java Runtime Engine (JRE)

It is an environment that is required for executing a java application. A very popular usage of JRE is with a browser where it is available as a plugin to allow applet (client side program) to execute. JRE is composed of following components:

a. Interpreter: It understand binary java code (e.g.: java.exe).
b. Tools: They provide various functionality such as security, core services, internationalization, RMI etc.
   (e.g.: keytool, rmiregistry, javacpl etc)
c. Library: Java Application Programming Interface (rt.jar, jce.jar, jsse.jar etc.)

JRE cannot be used for development of Java application but it is used for executing them.

Java Development Kit (JDK)

It is an environment that is targeted for developers who desire to develop Java applications. JDK is nothing but Java Standard Edition which is used for development of desktop, user interface, communication and applet types of applications. JDK is composed of following components:

a. Compiler: It is used to compile java code to bytecode (e.g Javac.exe).
b. Interpreter: It processes bytecode to native code (e.g. java.exe).
c. Tools: They provide functionality such as RMI, internationalization, core services, security.
d. Library: Reusable pre-defined Java API (rt.jar, jce.jar, jsse.jar etc.).

JDK is a super set of JRE. JDK has all the components that JRE has plus it has a compiler.

Installing JDK

JDK can be downloaded from
http://www.oracle.com/technetwork/java/javase/downloads/jdk8-downloads-2133151.html.

JDK is available for many operating systems such as Windows, Linux, Mac OS, and Solaris etc. When downloading ensure you choose Java 8 with latest update. It is very important to choose the right architecture for JRE is available for 32/64 bit architecture. After JDK is downloaded double click on it to install it. Choose the default options to complete the installation.
On Windows OS 32 bit Java will install in – C:\Program Files (x86)\Java\Jdk1.8.xxx folder and
On 64 bit Windows OS Java will install in - C:\Program Files\Java\Jdk1.8.xxx folder.

Please ensure that you have downloaded JDK and installed it. Please don't download JRE and install it.

Installing Notepad++

It is general purpose code editor that has support for over 20 programming languages. The latest version is v6.9 .The editor can be downloaded from https://notepad-plus-plus.org/download/v6.9.html

Summary

JDK is the minimum environment required for a developer for developing Java applications. JDK can be downloaded from oracle website. JDK is the super set of JRE.

Chapter 3
Setting PATH Variable

<u>Topics</u>
- ✓ **Introduction**
- ✓ **What is PATH variable?**
- ✓ **Summary**

Introduction

Environment variables are special Windows OS variables that are dynamic in nature. They contain values that can be used by programs. Environment variables are used for identify installation directory, location of temporary files, tools and profile settings. The value of environment variable is changeable and updateable therefore environment variable is called as dynamic.

Some of the common environment variables are
   a. %appdata%: Location of Application Data folder for your user profile.
   b. %commonprogramfiles%: Location of Common Files folder, within the main Program Files folder.
   c. %path%: Location of various tools e.g. Java tools.
   d. %programfiles%: Location of where programs are installed.
   e. %temp%: Location of temporary files.
   f. %windir%: Location of windows system files.

"SET" command provide a complete list of all environment variables from command line.

```
C:\>SET
ALLUSERSPROFILE=C:\ProgramData
APPDATA=C:\Users\PC\AppData\Roaming
asl.log=Destination=file
CommonProgramFiles=C:\Program Files\Common Files
CommonProgramFiles(x86)=C:\Program Files (x86)\Common Files
CommonProgramW6432=C:\Program Files\Common Files
COMPUTERNAME=PC
ComSpec=C:\Windows\system32\cmd.exe
FP_NO_HOST_CHECK=NO
GTK_BASEPATH=C:\Program Files (x86)\GtkSharp\2.12\
HOMEDRIVE=C:
HOMEPATH=\Users\PC
LOCALAPPDATA=C:\Users\PC\AppData\Local
LOGONSERVER=\\PC
NUMBER_OF_PROCESSORS=4
OS=Windows_NT
Path=C:\ProgramData\Oracle\Java\javapath;C:\Windows\system32;C:\Windows;C:\Windo
ws\System32\Wbem;C:\Windows\System32\WindowsPowerShell\v1.0\;C:\Program Files\Mi
crosoft SQL Server\120\Tools\Binn\;C:\Windows\system32\config\systemprofile\.dnx
\bin;C:\Program Files\Microsoft DNX\Dnvm\;C:\Program Files (x86)\nodejs\;C:\Prog
ram Files (x86)\Windows Kits\10\Windows Performance Toolkit\;C:\Program Files\Mi
crosoft SQL Server\Client SDK\ODBC\110\Tools\Binn\;C:\Program Files (x86)\Micros
oft SQL Server\120\Tools\Binn\;C:\Program Files\Microsoft SQL Server\120\DTS\Bin
n\;C:\Program Files (x86)\Microsoft SQL Server\120\Tools\Binn\ManagementStudio\;
C:\Program Files (x86)\Microsoft SQL Server\120\DTS\Binn\;C:\Program Files (x86)
\GtkSharp\2.12\bin;C:\Users\PC\AppData\Roaming\npm;C:\Program Files\Java\jdk1.8.
0_65\bin
```

"SET" followed by environment variable will show value for that variable only.

```
C:\>set PATH
Path=C:\ProgramData\Oracle\Java\javapath;C:\Windows\system32;C:\Windows;C:\Windo
ws\System32\Wbem;C:\Windows\System32\WindowsPowerShell\v1.0\;C:\Program Files\Mi
crosoft SQL Server\120\Tools\Binn\;C:\Windows\system32\config\systemprofile\.dnx
\bin;C:\Program Files\Microsoft DNX\Dnvm\;C:\Program Files (x86)\nodejs\;C:\Prog
ram Files (x86)\Windows Kits\10\Windows Performance Toolkit\;C:\Program Files\Mi
crosoft SQL Server\Client SDK\ODBC\110\Tools\Binn\;C:\Program Files (x86)\Micros
oft SQL Server\120\Tools\Binn\;C:\Program Files\Microsoft SQL Server\120\DTS\Bin
n\;C:\Program Files (x86)\Microsoft SQL Server\120\Tools\Binn\ManagementStudio\;
C:\Program Files (x86)\Microsoft SQL Server\120\DTS\Binn\;C:\Program Files (x86)
\GtkSharp\2.12\bin;C:\Users\PC\AppData\Roaming\npm;C:\Program Files\Java\jdk1.8.
0_65\bin
PATHEXT=.COM;.EXE;.BAT;.CMD;.VBS;.VBE;.JS;.JSE;.WSF;.WSH;.MSC
```

Setting "PATH" Variable

The "PATH" variable contain the location of tools, specifically it identifies the location of java interpreter (Java.exe), Java compiler (Javac.exe) and Java tool chain.

PATH variable can be set in two ways using
   a. Command Line
   b. Control Panel

Command Line Setting

The PATH variable can be set using SET command. The SET command is not case sensitive. This technique will apply only for the current command line session. Let's see how to set PATH variable at command line.

e.g.

Set path= "C:\Program Files\Java\jdk1.8.0_65\bin"
Explanation: The above command will overwrite the PATH variable with the location of JDK 1.8.Use double quotes for directory that contain space. When setting PATH variable do not specify the name of tool only identify the location.

Set PATH = "C:\Program Files\Java\jdk1.8.0_65\bin"
Explanation: Path variable is case insensitive. The directory is also case sensitive.

Set PATH = %path%; "C:\Program Files\Java\jdk1.8.0_65\bin"
Explanation: The above command will append the location of PATH variable.

Setting PATH Using Control Panel
This is a superior way of setting PATH variable because it will be permanent.
To set the PATH variable using control panel follows the steps below.

a. Start control panel -> Choose System applet.
b. Click Advanced System Settings.
c. Choose advanced tab from environment variables dialog box.
d. Click on Environment variables button.
e. Goto Path variable in System Variables container and edit values to it.
f. If PATH variable is not available then create a new PATH variable and add value to it.

Summary
Path environment variable identifies the location of Java compiler and Java interpreter. Path can be set from command line or control panel. Control panel technique is better than command line because it is permanent.

Chapter 4
Java Compiler and Java Interpreter

Topics
- ✓ **Introduction**
- ✓ **Java Compiler**
- ✓ **Java Interpreter**
- ✓ **Summary**

Introduction
The most fundamental tools that a Java programmer use are the Java compiler (Javac.exe) and Java interpreter (Java.exe). The PATH environment should be set to the location of the JDK bin folder which contain the compiler and the interpreter. If you not sure that your PATH is not set, refer to the previous chapter on PATH environment variable.

Java Compiler
The Java compiler is used for compiling Java programs. The compilation process generate bytecode. Bytecode is binary code that is understood by Java Virtual Machine (JVM).
The Java compiler can be activated by using "Javac.exe" command at command line.

Some of compiler options are:
   a. -help: Display all the compiler option.
   b. -version: Returns the compiler version.
   c. -verbose: Output compiler messages.
   d. –deprecation: Identify retired APIs.
   e. –nowarn: Generate no warnings.

The compiler options are case sensitive.

A snapshot of Java compiler options.

```
C:\>javac
Usage: javac <options> <source files>
where possible options include:
  -g                         Generate all debugging info
  -g:none                    Generate no debugging info
  -g:{lines,vars,source}     Generate only some debugging info
  -nowarn                    Generate no warnings
  -verbose                   Output messages about what the compiler is doing
  -deprecation               Output source locations where deprecated APIs are used
  -classpath <path>          Specify where to find user class files and annotation process
ors
  -cp <path>                 Specify where to find user class files and annotation process
ors
  -sourcepath <path>         Specify where to find input source files
  -bootclasspath <path>      Override location of bootstrap class files
  -extdirs <dirs>            Override location of installed extensions
  -endorseddirs <dirs>       Override location of endorsed standards path
  -proc:{none,only}          Control whether annotation processing and/or compilation is d
one.
  -processor <class1>[,<class2>,<class3>...] Names of the annotation processors to run; by
passes default discovery process
  -processorpath <path>      Specify where to find annotation processors
  -parameters                Generate metadata for reflection on method parameters
  -d <directory>             Specify where to place generated class files
  -s <directory>             Specify where to place generated source files
  -h <directory>             Specify where to place generated native header files
  -implicit:{none,class}     Specify whether or not to generate class files for implicitly
referenced files
  -encoding <encoding>       Specify character encoding used by source files
  -source <release>          Provide source compatibility with specified release
  -target <release>          Generate class files for specific VM version
  -profile <profile>         Check that API used is available in the specified profile
  -version                   Version information
  -help                      Print a synopsis of standard options
  -Akey[=value]              Options to pass to annotation processors
```

Java Interpreter

It is used for executing Java programs i.e. the interpreter take bytecode as an input and execute that code by converting it to native code. The Java interpreter is identified by "Java.exe" command.

Some of the command Java interpreter options are:
  a. -version: display interpreter version.
  b. -verbose: display interpreter information.
  c. -help: display interpreter options.

The interpreter options are case sensitive.
A snapshot of Java interpreter options

```
C:\>java
Usage: java [-options] class [args...]
          (to execute a class)
   or  java [-options] -jar jarfile [args...]
          (to execute a jar file)
where options include:
    -d32          use a 32-bit data model if available
    -d64          use a 64-bit data model if available
    -server       to select the "server" VM
                  The default VM is server.

    -cp <class search path of directories and zip/jar files>
    -classpath <class search path of directories and zip/jar files>
                  A ; separated list of directories, JAR archives,
                  and ZIP archives to search for class files.
    -D<name>=<value>
                  set a system property
    -verbose:[class|gc|jni]
                  enable verbose output
    -version      print product version and exit
    -version:<value>
                  Warning: this feature is deprecated and will be removed
                  in a future release.
                  require the specified version to run
    -showversion  print product version and continue
    -jre-restrict-search | -no-jre-restrict-search
                  Warning: this feature is deprecated and will be removed
                  in a future release.
                  include/exclude user private JREs in the version search
    -? -help      print this help message
    -X            print help on non-standard options
    -ea[:<packagename>...|:<classname>]
```

Summary

The Java compiler is activted using "Javac.exe" command.It is used used for compiling Java programs.The Java interpreter is called using "Java.exe" command. It is used for executing Java programs.

15

Chapter 5
First Program

<u>Topics</u>
- ✓ **Introduction**
- ✓ **The First Program**
- ✓ **Comments**
- ✓ **Summary**

Introduction

A Java program is saved with .java extension. The extension is case sensitive. The Java program is compiled using the Java compiler (javac.exe) and executed using Java interpreter (java.exe)

The First Program

Let's write our first Java program and save it as Prg.ca. A Java program that does not have valid extension (.java) the java compiler generate an error.

```
// Name: Prg.ca
// Description: A valid Java program has .java as an extension
class Program {
}
```

Compilation Command: Javac Prg.ca

Output:

```
error: Class names, 'Prg.ca', are only accepted if annotation processing is explicitly requested
1 error
```

If a Java program is saved with .jAva extension then also the compiler will generate an error because the file extension is case sensitive.

```
// Name: Prg.jAva
// Description: The extension of the Java program is case sensitive.
// The correct extension is .java
class Program {

}
```

Compilation Command: Javac Prg.jAva
Output:

```
error: Class names, 'Prg.jAva', are only accepted if annotation processing is explicitly requested
1 error
```

16

A valid extension for Java program is .java. The compiler generate a .class file as part of compilation process. The .class file contain binary instructions called as bytecode which are interpreted by Java interpreter. Now let's write a correct named Java program and investigate the bytecode.

// Description: A valid java program has .java as an extension.
// Bytecode is binary java instruction.
// Save this program as Prg2.java

class Program {

}

The above program when compiled will generate a .class file named as Prg2.class. This code does not execute as it does not have "main" method which is the entry point in a program. Bytecode is binary code that can only be understood by Java interpreter. Open Prg2.class file in an editor to examine it.

```
Êþº¾    4
  L



   -<init>   └()V  ┘Code   #LineNumberTable
SourceFile      Prg2.java
  ┘ |    program  ┼java/lang/Object
  ┐ └         ┘ |    ─              |*·  ±            ─          ▯   ┐
```

Comments
The comments in a Java program can be given in two ways
    a. Single line - // This is a comment
    b. Multi line –
          /*
               This comment spans
               Across multiple
               lines
          */

Summary
A Java program has .java as an extension. The Java program compile bytecode. Bytecode is processed by Java interpreter.

Chapter 6
The HelloWorld Program

<u>Topics</u>
  - ✓ **Introduction**
  - ✓ **The HelloWorld Program**
  - ✓ **Summary**

Introduction
An executable Java program has a "main" method of valid signature which act as entry point for the program. The "main" method has to be encapsulated within a class.

The HelloWorld Program
Let's write a HelloWorld Program. After writing the program compile it using Javac.exe (compiler) and use Java.exe (interpreter) to execute it.

```
//Prg.java
// Description: HelloWorld Program

class Program {
 public static void main(String args[]) {
   System.out.println("Namaskar - HelloWorld - Java");
  }
}
```

Command at command line:
  a. Javac Prg.java
  b. Java Program

Output:
```
Namaskar - HelloWorld - Java
```


Try-Out:
  a. Make main method upper case.
     Result: Compiler error.

The valid "main" methods that can be used in a Java are
  a. public static void main(String[] args).
  b. public static void main(String args[]).
  c. public static void main(String ...a).

Only one of the above "main" method can be used in a class at a time.

Let's verify the above with help of examples.

```
//Prg2.java
//Description: Helloworld program using "main(String[] args)" method as entry point
class Program {
 public static void main(String[] args) {
   System.out.println("Namaskar - HelloWorld - Java");
  }
}
```

Output:
```
Namaskar - HelloWorld - Java
```

```
//Prg3.java
//Description : Using "main(String ...a)" method as entry point.

class Program {
 public static void main(String ...a) {
   System.out.println("Namaskar - HelloWorld - Java");
  }
}
```

Output:
```
Namaskar - HelloWorld - Java
```

Explanation:
   a. "main(String ...a)" represent Java syntax that informs the compiler to allow any number of string arguments to main method.

Try out:
   a. Have a main method which does not have valid signature.
      Result: Program will compile but will not execute.

Summary
Main method is the entry point in a program only when it is of a valid signature else it behave like an ordinary method of the class.

Chapter 7
Anatomy of HelloWorld Program

Introduction
In this chapter you will understand the anatomy of the HelloWorld program.

Command Line Arguments
The main method is an entry point which take a string array as an argument. The arrays are bounds checked in Java. The programmer can pass any type of data at command line to main method. The data passed will be captured as string. Programmer has to perform type conversion for further processing on that data.

Let's understand how to pass command line arguments and capture them in our program.
```
//Prg.java
//Description: Passing and capturing command line arguments

class Program {
 public static void main(String args[]) {
   System.out.println("HelloWorld :" + args[0]);
   System.out.println("HelloWorld " + args[0] +"," + args[1]);
 }
}
```
Output:

```
D:\>javac Prg.java

D:\>java Program Ram Hari
HelloWorld :Ram
HelloWorld Ram,Hari
```

When the programmer passes just "Ram" as an argument. The Java interpreter throws Array Exception because array is bounds checked i.e. the program is anticipating 2 arguments.

Output:

```
D:\>javac Prg.java

D:\>java Program Ram
HelloWorld :Ram
Exception in thread "main" java.lang.ArrayIndexOutOfBoundsException: 1
        at Program.main(Prg.java:6)
```

Now let's understand the behavior of main method better by passing Integers. All arguments passed to main method are accepted as String. If integer is passed then it has to be converted for further processing. The next program explain how to accomplish this.

```
//Prg2.java
//Description: Passing integers at command line

class Program {
 public static void main(String args[]) {
        int i = Integer.parseInt(args[0]); // conversion of string to integer
        int j = Integer.parseInt(args[1]);
        System.out.println("The sum is :" + (i+j));
 }
}
```

Output:

```
D:\>javac Prg2.java

D:\>java Program 10 20
The sum is :30
```

If one of the argument that is passed is character then Java interpreter raises an exception. This is because character cannot be converted to integer

Output:
```
D:\>javac Prg2.java

D:\>java Program 10 A
Exception in thread "main" java.lang.NumberFormatException: For input string: "A"
        at java.lang.NumberFormatException.forInputString(Unknown Source)
        at java.lang.Integer.parseInt(Unknown Source)
        at java.lang.Integer.parseInt(Unknown Source)
        at Program.main(Prg2.java:4)
```

Main Method
The signature of the main method cannot be changed i.e "void" cannot precede "static" keyword if void appears before static compiler will report an error.

The access specifier of "main" method can only be public i.e. it cannot be protected,private or default. Let's understand the behaviour of main method with help of an example.

```
//Prg3.java
//Desription: Using main method signature

class Program { // Compiler Error
 public void static main(String args[]){  // static should precede void
  System.out.println("Namaskar Helloworld Java");
 }
}
```

Output:

```
Prg3.java:4: error: <identifier> expected
 public void static main(String args[]){
             ^
Prg3.java:4: error: '(' expected
 public void static main(String args[]){
             ^
Prg3.java:4: error: invalid method declaration; return type required
 public void static main(String args[]){
                    ^
3 errors
```

When a main method is not public then it won't be an entry point in the program. If main method is non-public the compiler won't report any error but interpreter will raise an exception this is because interpreter does not find any entry point hence it cannot execute the program.

```
//Prg4.java
//Description: Using main method signature - access specifier
class Program {
 protected static void main(String args[]){
  System.out.println("Namaskar Helloworld Java");
 }
}
```

Output:

```
Error: Main method not found in class Program, please define the main method as:
   public static void main(String[] args)
or a JavaFX application class must extend javafx.application.Application
```

Anatomy of System.out.println()
The System is a class which belong to "java.lang" package. A package is a repositry of

reusable, organized Java code. The "java.lang" is the default package hence it is not required to be imported.

The "out" is a pubic static object of PrintStream class. Static objects are class level hence can be accessed without an instance of the class.

The "println" is a method that belong to PrintStream class that prints data on Stanard Output i.e Visual Display Unit (Monitor).

Summary
Main method takes string array as an argument.Main method has to be public only.
The "java.lang" is the default package in Java.

Chapter 8
Multiple Main Methods

<u>Topics</u>
- ✓ **Introduction**
- ✓ **Multiple main Methods in a Single Class**
- ✓ **Multiple Classes and main Method**
- ✓ **Summary**

Introduction
A Java program can have multiple classes. When a Java program that has multiple classes is compiled it will produce many .class files i.e. each class in Java program will compile to a specific class file. The name of .class file will be same as the name of the class in the program.

Since Java has support for method overloading (mechanism where a class can have many methods with same name but which differ in signature) a class can have any number of main methods but one and only one main method will be the entry point for that class. Basically we can have many classes and each class can have one main method as entry point.

Multiple main Methods in a Single Class
A class in Java can have any number of main methods as Java has support for Method Overloading (mechanism where a class can have many methods with same name but which differ in signature) but there can only be one Entry point main method which is of specific pre-defined signature (refer Chapter 6). Let's understand how to create multiple main methods in a single class with the help of an example.

```
//Prg.java
//Description: Multiple Main methods in a single class

class Program {
    public static void main(String args[]) {   // This is the entry point
        System.out.println("Namaskar - Helloworld - Java");
    }
    /* public static void main(String ... args) {
        System.out.println("");
    }
    */
    public static void main() {        // This is not entry point
        System.out.println ("Main() method");
    }
```

```
        public void main(String ar) {      // This is not entry point
                System.out.println("String argument-main");
        }
}
```

The above program compile and execute without any error
Output:

```
Namaskar - Helloworld - Java
```

If the commented code is uncommented then compiler yield into an error because there can only be one entry point within a class.
Output:

```
Prg.java:9: error: cannot declare both main(String...) and main(String[]) in Program
        public static void main(String ... args) {
                          ^
1 error
```

Multiple Classes and main Method

A Java program can have multiple classes and each class can have only one entry point but the class can have many main methods which do not act as entry point. Each class in the program will compile to a .class file.

To execute a specific main method issue the command "Java <classname>".

Let's understand how to create main methods in multiple classes.

```
//Prg2.java
//Description : Multiple classes in a program

class Program {
 public static void main(String args[] ) { // This is the entry point
    System.out.println("Program class - Main method");
 }
 public static void main() { // This is not entry point
        System.out.println ("Program class - Main() method");
 }

 public void main(String ar) { // This is not entry point
        System.out.println("Program class - String argument-main");
 }
}

class Test {
        public static void main(String[] args) { // This is the entry point
                System.out.println("Test class - Main method");
        }
        public static void main() { // This is not entry point
                System.out.println ("Test class-Main() method");
```

```
        }

        public void main(String ar) { // This is not entry point
                System.out.println("Test2 class-String argument-main");
        }
}

class Test2 {
        public static void main(String[] args) { // This is the entry point
                System.out.println("Test2 class - Main method");
        }
        public static void main() { // This is not entry point
                System.out.println ("Test2 class - Main() method");
        }

        public void main(String ar) { // This is not entry point
                System.out.println("Test2 class-String argument-main");
        }
}
```

To execute a desired main method used the command : Java <classname>.
Output:
   a. Java Program

```
Program class - Main method
```

   b. Java Test

```
Test class - Main method
```

   c. Java Test2

```
Test2 class - Main method
```

Summary
A class can only have one entry point.A program can contain multiple classes and each class
can have it's own entry point. Each class compile to an individual class file.

Chapter 9
Public Class and File Name

<u>**Topics**</u>
- ✓ **Introduction**
- ✓ **Public Class in a Program**
- ✓ **Summary**

Introduction
In this chapter we will discuss about how to rules of naming a java program and class or classes that are in it.

Public Class in a Program
A class can only have one of the two access specifiers i.e. a class can be declared with public or default (package level) access specifier.A class cannot be declared as private or protected.

There are rules that have to be followed when decarling a class or giving name to Java program(file).
- a. There can only be one public class per java file.
- b. The public class name and java file name has to be same.
- c. Even the cases have to match between the java file (name) and class (name).

Let's understand these rules with help of a program.

```
//Prg.java
//Description: Class cannot be declared as private or protected

public class Prg { // The name of the public class and file name have to be same
              // The name of program will be Prg.java
 public static void main(string args[]) {
  System.out.println("Namaste Java");
 }
}

class Test {
        public static void main(string args[]) {
             System.out.println("Test class");
        }
}
Command : Java Prg
Output:
Namaste Java
```

If the Test class is declared as private the compiler will report and error.
Output:

```
Prg.java:10: error: modifier private not allowed here
private class Test {
        ^
1 error
```

Summary
A class cannot be declared as private or protected. There can only be one public class per java file.

Chapter 10
Runtime Execution

<u>Topics</u>
- ✓ **Introduction**
- ✓ **Role of Java Interpreter**
- ✓ **What is JIT Compilation?**
- ✓ **Platform Independence**
- ✓ **Summary**

Introduction
In this chapter we will discuss about behaviour of program during runtime i.e. when the program is executing. We will also discuss about the role of interpreter.Understand what is JIT and learn about what makes Java platform independent.

Role of Java Interpreter
The interpreter can be activated by executing the command "Java.exe" from command line. The interpreter is also called as JVM (Java Virtual Machine). The responsibility of the interpreter are as follows:
- a. Taking bytecode as an input.
- b. Processing bytecode to native code(executable code for specific OS).
- c. Executing the native code.

What is JIT Compilation?
JIT stands for Just In Time compilation.It is an action performed by JVM where Bytecode is converted to Native code. Since it occur on demand hence it is called as Just In Time.

A diagram representing Just In Time Compilation.

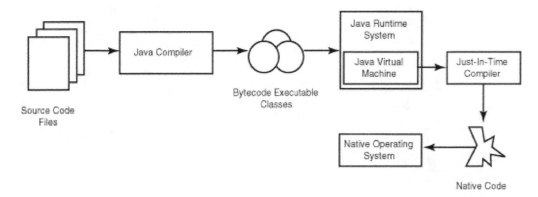

Platform Independence
A program is called platform independent when the binary code is not native and does not target a specific OS. Since Java Program is compiled into bytecode which does not target any OS but the bytecode is processed only by JVM and there are JVMs that are available for

different OS. This is what make Java program platform independent.
A diagram representing how Java is platform independent.

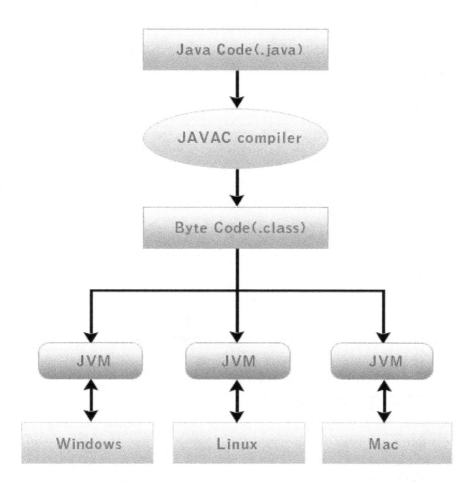

Summary
Java Virtual Machine is also called as pseudo OS.JVM convert bytecode to nativecode.Conversion of Bytecode to Nativecode is called JIT.

Chapter 11
Alternate HelloWorld Program

Introduction
In this chapter we will discuss an alternative way of printing data on screen i.e. printing data without using System.out.println() method.To accomplish this I will use the PrintStream class.

Using PrintStream Class
To create an object of PrintStream class we have to pass OutputStream object to the constructor of PrintStream class. The handle to output stream is established using FileDescriptor class 'out' field which is passed as an argument to FileOutputStream(child class of OutputStream class) class constructor. Let's understand this with the help of an example. Java.io package has to be imported as the classes used are available in that package.

```java
//Prg.java
//Description : Alternate HellWorld Program

import java.io.*;
class Program {
 public static void main(String args[]) {
        FileOutputStream obj = new FileOutputStream(FileDescriptor.out);
        PrintStream obj2 = new PrintStream(obj);
        obj2.println("Alternative Namaste Java");
 }
}
```

Output:

```
Alternative Namaste Java
```

Summary
FileDescriptor.out property identifies the standard output.PrintStream takes OuputStream class object when it is created.

Chapter 12
Numeric DataTypes

<u>Topics</u>
- ✓ **Introduction**
- ✓ **What is a Variable?**
- ✓ **Category of DataTypes**
- ✓ **Integer Types**
- ✓ **Floating Point Types**
- ✓ **Summary**

Introduction
In this chapter I will discuss how to create and use numeric variables. You will learn about creating and using Integer and Floating data types.

What is a Variable?
It is a memory location in a process that store data.Since Java is statically typed language the type of a variable is known at compile time therefore variable has a type. The core data types are also called as primitives. The primitives data types supported by Java are
- a. char
- b. byte
- c. short
- d. int
- e. long
- f. float
- g. double
- h. boolean

Based on the data type of the variable memory will be allocated by the JVM.

Category Of DataTypes
Broadly Java support two kinds of types
- Primitive data types – They are core data types
- Reference/Object data types – They derive from Object class directly or indirectly.

Integer Types
Since Java is statically typed, a variable has to be declared before usage.Integer type can only contain a whole number.The default integer type is 'int'. Supported integer types are

Data Type	Size(Bytes)	Sign
byte	1	Signed
short	2	Signed

int	4	Signed
long	8	Signed

Let's understand how to use integer types with help of an example.
//Prg.java
//Description : Integer data type behaviour

```java
class Program {
 public static void show() {
  byte b=12;
  short sh= 124;
  int i = 256;
  long l = 459;
  System.out.println("Byte value :"+b);
  System.out.println("Short value :"+sh);
  System.out.println("Int value :"+ i);
  System.out.println("Long value :" + l);
 }
 public static void main(String args[]){
   show();
 }
}
```

Output:
```
Byte value :12
Short value :124
Int value :256
Long value :459
```

//Prg2.java
//Description : Checking integer data type value range

```java
class Program {
 public static void show() {
  byte b=-128;  // -128 to 127 (inclusive)
  short sh= 124; //  -32,768 to 32,767
  int i = 256; //  -2^31 and a maximum value of 2^31-1
  long l = 459; //  -2^63 to 2^63-1

  System.out.println("Byte value :"+b);
  System.out.println("Short value :"+sh);
  System.out.println("Int value :"+ i);
  System.out.println("Long value :" + l);
```

```
}
public static void main(String args[]){
  show();
}
}
```

Output:
```
Byte value :-128
Short value :124
Int value :256
Long value :459
```

If byte variable is assigned value of -129 it will generate a compiler output.

```
Prg2.java:6: error: incompatible types: possible lossy conversion from int to byte
  byte b=-129;  // -128 to 127 (inclusive)
         ^
1 error
```

Floating Types
The floating numeric types can hold fractional number. Java has support for 2 floating types i.e. float and double. The float type has to be suffixed with 'f' because default floating type is double.

Data Type	Size(Bytes)	Sign
float	4	Signed
double	8	Signed

Let's understand the usage of floating types with help of examples.

```
//Prg3.java
//Description : Checking floating data type

class Program {
 public static void show() {
   float f = 10.10f; // identify a floating value by a suffix 'f'
   double d = 20.20d; // suffix 'd' for double is optional

   System.out.println("Byte value :"+f);
   System.out.println("Short value :"+d);
 }
 public static void main(String args[]){
   show();
 }
```

Output:

```
Byte value :10.1
Short value :20.2
```

If floating variable value is not suffixed with 'f', compiler will generate an error.

Output:

```
Prg3.java:6: error: incompatible types: possible lossy conversion from double to float
    float f = 10.10; // identify a floating value by a suffix 'f'
              ^
1 error
```

Using floating and integer types together.

```java
//Prg4.java
//Description: Using float and integer type together


class Program {
 public static void intOps() {
        int i=10;
        byte b=34;
        i= i*b;
        System.out.println("i= i*b :" + i);
 }

 public static void fltOps() {
        float f = 10.45f;
        double d = 45.5d;
        d = f*d;
        System.out.println("d = f*d :" + d);
 }
 public static void mixedOps() {
  float f = 10.10f;
  int j =10;
  f = f * j;
  System.out.println("f = f * j :" + f);
 }
 public static void main(String args[]){
        intOps();
        fltOps();
        mixedOps();
 }
}
```

Inference
    a. Higher memory type can hold result of an expression.
    b. Floating point can hold result of a mixed expression (integer cannot).

Output:

```
i= i*b :340
d = f*d :475.4749913215637
f = f * j :101.0
```

If result of an expression is held into a variable that cannot hold the value, compiler will a generate an error.
//Prg4a.java
//Description: Using float and integer type together


```java
class Program {
 public static void intOps() {
        int i=10;
        byte b=34;
        b= i*b;
        System.out.println("i= i*b :" + i);
 }

 public static void fltOps() {
        float f = 10.45f;
        double d = 45.5d;
        d = f*d;
        System.out.println("d = f*d :" + d);
 }
 public static void mixedOps() {
  float f = 10.10f;
  int j =10;
  j = f * j;
  System.out.println("f = f * j :" + f);
 }
 public static void main(String args[]){
        intOps();
        fltOps();
        mixedOps();
 }
}
```

Output:

```
Prg4a.java:9: error: incompatible types: possible lossy conversion from int to byte
        b= i*b;
           ^
Prg4a.java:22: error: incompatible types: possible lossy conversion from float to int
  j = f * j;
        ^
2 errors
```

A floating expression can be casted into int using the syntax
*int k= (int) f * f;*

//Prg5.java
//Description : Type casting float to an int

class Program {
public static void mixedOps() {
float f = 10.10f;
int j =10;
*j = (int) f * j;*
*System.out.println("j = (int) f * j :" + j);*
}
public static void main(String args[]){
mixedOps();
}
}

Output:
```
j = (int) f * j   :100
```

All variables in Java have default values unlike C or C++. Let's understand this better with help of an example.

//Prg6.java
//Description : Default value of numeric data types.

class Program {
byte b;
short sh;
int i;
long l;
float f;
double d;

public void show() {
System.out.println("Byte :"+b);
System.out.println("Short :"+sh);
System.out.println("Int :"+ i);
System.out.println("Long :"+ l);

```
            System.out.println("Float :"+ f);
            System.out.println("Double :"+ d);
        }

public static void main(String args[]) {
        Program obj = new Program();
        obj.show();

    }
}
```

Output:

```
Byte :0
Short :0
Int :0
Long :0
Float :0.0
Double :0.0
```

Summary

Java is statically typed language.DataTypes can be divided into 2 categories i.e. Primitive and Reference types.The default floating data type is double.

Chapter 13
Non Numeric DataTypes

Topics
- ✓ **Introduction**
- ✓ **Non Numeric Primitive Types?**
- ✓ **Non Numeric Reference Types**
- ✓ **Summary**

Introduction
In this chapter I will discuss how to use non-numeric data types. You will learn about how to use boolean, char and reference(non primitive) types.

Non Numeric Primitive Types
There two non numeric primitive types i.e char and boolean.

Data Type	Size(Bytes)
char	2
boolean	1

Let's understand this with help of an example.

```java
//Prg.java
//Description: Using char and boolean types

class Program {
  char c;
  boolean b;
 public void defValue() {
  System.out.println("Default Character value : "+ c);
  System.out.println("Default Boolean value :" + b);
 }

 public void show() {
  char i= 'a';
  boolean b = true;
  System.out.println("Character value : "+ i);
  System.out.println("Boolean value :" + b);
 }
 public static void main(String args[]) {
  Program obj = new Program();
  obj.defValue();
```

```
    obj.show();
  }
}
```

Ouput:

```
Default Character value :
Default Boolean value :false
Character value : a
Boolean value :true
```

Non Numeric Reference Type
Non Numeric reference type supported in Java are String and Object.String is aggregation of characters.Object is the mother class of all classes directly or indirectly.Let's understand this better with help of an example.

```
//Prg2.java
//Description : Non Numeric reference type behaviour


class Program {  // Program class inherit from Object class implicitly
  static void dataOps() {
    String str="Namaskar";
    Object obj="Vanakkam"; // Object is the mother class of all classes in java
    System.out.println ("String :" + str);
    System.out.println ("Object(String) :" + obj);
    obj = 234; // Object can be assigned with any value because it is the Mother class
                  // of all classes.
    System.out.println ("Object(String) :" + obj);
    obj = false;
    System.out.println ("Object(boolean) :" + obj);
    obj = 234.7899;
    System.out.println ("Object(double) :" + obj);
  }
  public static void main(String args[]) {
    dataOps();
  }
}
```


Output:

```
String :Namaskar
Object(String) :Vanakkam
Object(String) :234
Object(boolean) :false
Object(double) :234.7899
```

Summary

Size of character data type is 2 bytes.Size of Boolean data type is 1 byte.

Chapter 14
Literals and Constants

Topics
- ✓ **Introduction**
- ✓ **Using Literals.**
- ✓ **Using Constants.**
- ✓ **Summary**

Introduction
In this chapter I will discuss about how to create and use Literals and Constants.

Using Literals
Fixed or constant value stored in a variable is called as a Literal. Literals can be used for all primitives that are supported by Java. Literals can also be used with reference type String. Literals can be used with Integer in 3 ways:

- a. Decimal : Start with number e.g. int I = 889;
- b. Octal : Start with '0' e.g. int i= 0123;
- c. Hexadecimal : Start with 0x/0X e.g. int i=0x1234;

Let's understand this better with help of an example.

```java
//Prg.java
//Description: Integer literal usage.

class Program {
  static void prgOps() {
        int i=234;
        int j=01;
        int k=0xa;
        System.out.println("\n int--");
        System.out.println("Decimal Literal :"+ i);
        System.out.println("Octal Literal :" + j);
        System.out.println("Hexadecimal Liternal :" + k);
  }

  static void prgOps2() {
        short i=2834;
        short j=071;
        short k=0xab;
        System.out.println("\n short--");
        System.out.println("Decimal Literal :"+ i);
```

```java
        System.out.println("Octal Literal :" + j);
        System.out.println("Hexadecimal Literal :" + k);
    }

public static void main(String args[]) {
    prgOps();
    prgOps2();
}
}
```

Output:

```
 int--
Decimal Literal :234
Octal Literal :1
Hexadecimal Literal :10

 short--
Decimal Literal :2834
Octal Literal :57
Hexadecimal Literal :171
```

If the hexadecimal is given incorrect value compiler reports an error.

```
Prg.java:8: error: hexadecimal numbers must contain at least one hexadecimal digit
        int k=0xgg;
              ^
Prg.java:8: error: not a statement
        int k=0xgg;
              ^
2 errors
```

The floating point literal is by default of type double. To identify a float type suffix 'f/F' after the value e.g. float f = 10.45f. If required identify a double suffix 'd/D' after the value e.g. double d= 45.231d.To identify powerof 'e' can be used. Let's understand this better with help of an example.

```java
//Prg2.java
// Description : Floating point literal usage

class Program {
    static void prgOps() {
        float i=234.3423f;
        double j=79879.345d;
        double k= 686868e4;
        System.out.println("Decimal Literal :"+ i);
```

```
            System.out.println("Octal Literal :" + j);
            System.out.println("Hexadecimal Liternal :" + k);
    }
  public static void main(String args[]) {
    prgOps();
  }
}
```

Output:

```
Decimal Literal :234.3423
Octal Literal :79879.345
Hexadecimal Liternal :6.86868E9
```

The character literal is enclosed in single quote and string literal is put in double quotes. The boolean type can have any of the 2 literal values i.e. true or false. Java also has support for null literal but it cannot be used with primitives but can be used with reference types.Let's understand it better with an example.

```
//Prg3.java
//Description : Literal usage with char,String and boolean type.

class Program {
  static void prgOps() {
        char c = 'a';
        String str = "Vanakkam Java";
        // c=null; // error cannot be used with primitives
        str = null;
        boolean b = true;
        // b= null; // error
        System.out.println("Char literal:"+c);
        System.out.println("String literal:"+str);
        System.out.println("Boolean literal:"+b);

  }
  public static void main(String args[]) {
    prgOps();
  }
}
```

Output:

```
Char literal:a
String literal:null
Boolean literal:true
```

Using Constants

Constant is a variable whose value once assigned cannot be changed.Constant variable is declared using 'final' keyword.
Usage

- final int i=10;
- final char c='a';
- final boolean b = true;

Let's understand this with help of an example.

```
//Prg4.java
//Description: Creating constant variable

class Program {
 public static void main(String args[]) {
   final int i=10; // final make a variable constant
   final float f= 10.10f;
   final double d = 20.20;
   final char c = 'a';
   final boolean b = true;
   final String str = "Namaste";


   System.out.println("i :"+i);
   System.out.println("f :"+f);
   System.out.println("d :"+d);
   System.out.println("c :"+c);
   System.out.println("b :"+b);
   System.out.println("str :"+str);
 }
}
```

Output:
```
i :10
f :10.1
d :20.2
c :a
b :true
str :Namaste
```

Summary

Fixed or constant value store in a variable is called a literal. Final keyword is used for making a variable constant.

Chapter 15
Escape Sequence

Introduction
In this chapter we will learn about Escape Sequence usage in Java. Escape Sequences are speical characters. They are also called as control sequences.

What is Escape Sequence?
It is used to provide alternative meaning to series of character. Escape sequence start with a backslash ('\'). It has special meaning for the compiler.Some of the escape sequence characters supported are:

a. \t - Insert a tab in the text.
b. \b - Insert a backspace in the text.
c. \n - Insert a newline in the text.
d. \r - Insert a carriage return in the text.
e. \f - Insert a formfeed in the text.
f. \' - Insert a single quote character in the text.
g. \" - Insert a double quote character in the text.
h. \\ - Insert a backslash character in the text.

Let's understand escape sequences with help of an example.

```
The                 tab escape sequence in action
T backspace escape sequence in action
The

 newline escape sequence in action
 carriage return escape sequence in action
The ♀♀ formfeed escape sequence in action
The ' single quote escape sequence in action
The " double quote escape sequence in action
The \ backslash escape sequence in action
```

Summary
'\r' is used for carriage return, '\n' is used for newline and '\t' is used for tab.

Chapter 16
Immutable String

Topics
✓ **Introduction**
✓ **What is Immutability?**
✓ **Using String type**
✓ **Summary**

Introduction
In this chapter I will discuss about the concept of Immutability and after that we will learn about how string data type is immutable.

What is Immutability?
The state of an object cannot be changed after initialization is called as Immutability. It should be very clear that immutablility does not mean constant an entity. An immutable object is an object where the internal fields cannot be changed after constructor call.Objects which are immutable cannot have their state changed after they have been created.

Using String Type
String is a reference type (it is not primitive).String is immutable.Once value is assigned to string variable it cannot be changed.If a string is assigned a new value then JVM will create a new string on heap memory.

Let's understand string immutablility with help of an example.

```
//Prg.java
//Description : String Immutable behaviour

class Program {
     static void immOps() {
       String s = "Namaste";
       s.concat(" Java"); // The new string is not concatenated
       System.out.println("Value of string after concat() :"+s);
     }
     static void immOps2() {
       String s = "Namaste";
       s=s.concat(" Java");
       System.out.println("Value of string after concat()(with assignment) :"+s);
     }

     public static void main(String args[]){
```

```
        immOps();
        immOps2();
    }
}
```

Output:

If programmer is not careful about using strings then this may lead to performance issues. If the string variable has to be intialized multiple times then it is best to use StringBuilder.

Strings can be compared in two ways i.e. by value and reference. String can be compared by value using equals method and by reference using == operator.Let's understand this better with help of an example.

```
//Prg2.java
//Description: String comparision

class Program {
    static void strOps() {
        String str = "Namaste";
        String str2 = "namaste";
        System.out.println("String are same(case sensitive) :"+ str2.equals(str));
        System.out.println("String are same(case insensitive) :" +
str.equalsIgnoreCase(str2));
    }

    static void strOps2() {
        String str = "Namaste";
        String str2 = "namaste";
        if (str==str2) { // Reference comparison
          System.out.println("Strings share same reference");
        } else {
          System.out.println("Strings do not share same reference");
        }
    }
    public static void main(String args[]) {
        strOps();
    }
}
```

Output:

```
String are same(case sensitive) :false
String are same(case insensitive) :true
```

Summary
String is immutable type. String can be compared as a value or as a reference.

Chapter 17
StringBuilder Class

Introduction
In this chapter we will discuss about how to use StringBuilder Class. This is a mechanism to initialize and reintialize strings without creating a new string in memory, in short StringBuilder is not immutable.

Using StringBuilder Class
It is a mutable sequence of characters.StringBuilder class is not immutable like String class. Key methods of StringBuilder class are
- Append()
- Insert()

The StringBuilder is available in java.io package hence it has to be imported.
Let's understand usage of StringBuilder class with help of an example.

```java
//Prg.java
//Description: Using StringBuilder class

import java.lang.*;

class Program {

  public static void main(String[] args) {

  StringBuilder str = new StringBuilder("Namaste");
  str.append(" Java");
  System.out.println("Using Append() method:" + str);
  str.insert(5," Vanakkam");
  System.out.println("Using Insert() method:" + str);
  str.delete(2,5);
  System.out.println("Using Delete() method: "+ str);

  }
}
```

Output:
```
Using Append() method:Namaste Java
Using Insert() method:Namas Vanakkamte Java
Using Delete() method: Na Vanakkamte Java
```

Summary

StringBuilder is mutable. Delete() method is used for removing characters from string.

Chapter 18
Wrapper Classes

Topics
- ✓ **Introduction**
- ✓ **Using Wrapper Class**
- ✓ **Autoboxing and Unboxing**
- ✓ **Summary**

Introduction
In this chapter you will learn about how to convert primitive data type into an object. This conversion happen with the help of wrapper classes. In this chapter I will also discuss about the concept of Autoboxing and Unboxing.

Using Wrapper Classes
Wrapper class is used for converting a core data type into an object.There are 8 wrapper classes for 8 data types.List of wrapper classes is as follows

Primitive Type	Wrapper Class
boolean	Boolean
char	Character
byte	Byte
short	Short
int	Integer
long	Long
float	Float
double	Double

Principally wrapper classes are used for
a. Representing data as null if required
b. Using the data in a collection.

Let's understand the usage of wrapper classes with help of an example.

```java
//Prg.java
//Description : Wrapper class usage

class Program {
    static void wrapperOps() {
        int i=10;
        Integer iw = Integer.valueOf(i); // int to Integer
        System.out.println("After conversion(primitive to wrapper) :"+ iw);
```

```
        int j = iw.intValue();
        System.out.println("After conversion(wrapper to primitive) :"+j);
    }

    public static void main(String args[]) {
wrapperOps();
    }
}
```

Output:

```
After conversion(primitive to wrapper) :10
After conversion(wrapper to primitive) :10
```

Autoboxing and Unboxing

Automatic conversion of primitive to equivalent wrapper type by compiler is called Autoboxing.

e.g.

```
int i=10;
Integer j=i;
```

Automatic conversion of wrapper type to equivalent primitive type by compiler is called Unboxing.

e.g.

```
Integer j= new Integer(50);
int i=j;
```

Let's understand this better with the help of an example.

```
//Prg2.java
//Description : Autoboxing and Unboxing behaviour

class Program {
    static void boxOps() {
        int i=20;
        Integer j=i; // Autoboxing
        Integer m = new Integer(77);
        int k=m; // Unboxing
        System.out.println("Value of i(primitive) :"+i);
        System.out.println("Value of j(wrapper - Autoboxing) :"+j);
        System.out.println("Value of k(primitive- Unboxing) :"+k);
    }
    public static void main(String args[]) {
        boxOps();
    }
}
```

Output:

```
Value of i(primitive) :20
Value of j(wrapper - Autoboxing) :20
Value of k(primitive- Unboxing) :77
```

A wrapper can only be automatically be converted to it's eqivalent type. If we try to convert to any other type compiler report and error.

......

```
//Code snapshot
        Integer m = new Integer(77);
        int k=m; // Unboxing
        short sh = m;  // compiler error
```

....

Output:

```
Prg2.java:10: error: incompatible types: Integer cannot be converted to short
            short sh = m;
                       ^
1 error
```

Summary

Wrapper class is used for representing data in a collection.Automatic conversion from primitive type to wrapper class is called Autoboxing and automatic conversion from wrapper class to primtive type is called as Unboxing.

Chapter 19
If...else

Topics
- ✓ **Introduction**
- ✓ **Using If. Else Statement**
- ✓ **Summary**

Introduction
In this chapter you will learn about how to use 'if' condition statement. The 'if' statement is used for checking conditions and making decision based on it.

Using If..else Statement
'If' is an fundamental and important construct in Java. It is used for making decision based on condition .

There are 3 flavours of 'if' construct
- if(condition)
- if(condition) <instructions> else <instructions>
- if(condition) <instructions> elseif <instructions> else <instructions>

The <condition> has to evaluate to a boolean 'true'. When more than one condition matches the execution the first matching conditon code is only executed other matching condition code will not be executed. Let's understand this with the help of an example.

```
//Prg.java
//Description: Using 'if' condition

class Program {
 static void ifOps() {
      int i=10;
      if (i > 5)
           System.out.println("i is greater than 5");
}

static void ifOps2() {
      boolean b=true;
      if (b)
           System.out.println("b is true");
      else
           System.out.println("b is false");
```

```
        }

    static void ifOps3() {
        int i=8;
        if (i == 5) // == is equality operator
            System.out.println("i value is 5");
        else if(i==6)
            System.out.println("i value is 5");
        else if(i==7)
            System.out.println("i value is 7");
        else
            System.out.println("The value of i is "+i);
    }


    public static void main(String args[]) {
        ifOps();
        ifOps2();
        ifOps3();
    }
}
```

Output:
```
i is greater than 5
b is true
The value of i is 8
```

The 'if' construct can only take a boolean condition, if the condition is not boolean then it would yield into a compiler error. The below code will yield into a compiler error

.... Code snapshot ....
```
    int i=8;
    if (i) // not a boolean condition
        System.out.println("i value is 5");
    else if(i==6)
        System.out.println("i value is 5");
    else if(i==7)
        System.out.println("i value is 7");
    else
        System.out.println("The value of i is "+i);
```
....

Ouput:

```
Prg.java:21: error: incompatible types: int cannot be converted to boolean
        if (i) // == is equality operator
            ^
1 error
```

Summary

'if' condition is used for decision making. Input for 'if' condition is a boolean and only first matching condition is executed.

Chapter 20
Switch. Case

Topics
- ✓ **Introduction**
- ✓ **Using Switch...case Statement**
- ✓ **Summary**

Introduction
In this chapter I will discuss about how to use Switch.. case statement. Switch..case is used for executing code based on a condition.

Using Switch..case Statement
Switch.. case is alternative to 'if .. else' statement. Switch statement can have any number of possible execution paths. A switch..case works with the following primitive types
- byte
- short
- char
- int

The 'case' has to have break statement else the control will fall through to next case. A switch..case can also have 'default' statement that will be executed when none of the case condition match.

Let's understand switch.. case with the help of an example.

In this example I show how to use integer with switch..case

```java
//Prg.java
//Description : Using Switch..case with integer

class Program {
 public static void switchOps() {
        int day=1;
        switch(day) {
                case 1:
                        System.out.println("Sunday");
                        break;
                case 2:
                        System.out.println("Monday");
                        break;
                case 3:
                        System.out.println("Tuesday");
                        break;
```

```java
            case 4:
                    System.out.println("Wednesday");
                    break;
            case 5:
                    System.out.println("Thursday");
                    break;
            case 6:
                    System.out.println("Thursday");
                    break;
            case 7:
                    System.out.println("Thursday");
                    break;
            default:
        System.out.println("Invalid day");
        }
}
public static void main(String args[]) {
    switchOps();
}
}
```

Output:
```
Sunday
```

If the value of 'day' variable is 9 then 'default' case will be executed.

Output:
```
Invalid day
```

If the value of the 'day' variable is 1 and 'case 1:' does not have break statement then the control will fall throught and code for 'case 2:' will also be executed.

Output:
```
Sunday
Monday
```

The next example demonstrate how to use char and String types inside swith..case.

```java
//Prg2.java
//Description : Using Switch..case with char & String

class Program {
 public static void switchOps() {
        char day='i';
```

```java
        switch(day) {
                case 'i':
                        System.out.println("One");
                        break;
                case 'x':
                        System.out.println("Ten");
                        break;
                default:
            System.out.println("Invalid number");
                }
}


        public static void switchOps2() {
          String state="TN";
          switch(state) {
                case "KA":
                        System.out.println("Karnataka");
                        break;
                case "TN":
                        System.out.println("Tamil Nadu");
                        break;
                default:
            System.out.println("Invalid state");
                }
}
 public static void main(String args[]) {
   switchOps();
   switchOps2();
 }
}
```

Output:
```
One
Tamil Nadu
```

Now let's learn about how to use enum inside switch..case.
//Prg3.java
//Description : Using enum with switch... case

```java
enum Metro {
        Delhi,
        Kolkata,
        Mumbai,
        Bengaluru
```

```
}

class Program {
    static void switchOps() {
        Metro city;
        city = Metro.Mumbai;
        switch(city) {
            case Delhi:
                System.out.println("Delhi is in north of India");
                break;
            case Mumbai:
                System.out.println("Mumbai is in west of India");
                break;
            case Kolkata:
                System.out.println("Kolkata is in east of India");
                break;
            case Bengaluru:
                System.out.println("Bengaluru is in south of India");
                break;
            default:
                System.out.println("This is not a metro city");
        }
    }
    public static void main(String args[]) {
        switchOps();
    }
}
```

Output:

```
Mumbai is in west of India
```

Summary

Switch.. case can work with primitives and reference types. 'break' keyword has to be used in "case" else logic will fall through. Enum can be used in switch case.

Chapter 21
For Loop

Topics
- ✓ **Introduction**
- ✓ **Using for. Loop**
- ✓ **Summary**

Introduction
In this chapter we will discuss about how to use for loop. The for loop helps in executing and iterating over instructions for a know number of times.

Using for...loop
It is used for executing a block of code multiple times(fixed).
Syntax

```
for (initialization; condition; increment) {
    instructions;
}
```

It has 3 parts
- Initialization : Is executed once at the beginning of the loop.
- Condition : Loop is executed only when condition evaluate to true.
- Increment : Variable can be incremented or decremented.

Let's understand this better with the help of an example

```
//Prg.java
//Description : Behaviour of for Loop
class Program {

    static void forOps() {
        for(int i=10; i>0;i--)
            System.out.println("Value of i :"+ i);
    }
    static void forOps2() {
        for(;;) {
            System.out.println("Infinite loop");
        }
    }
    public static void main(String args[]) {
        forOps();
        //forOps2();
    }
```

}
It is not mandtory to supply all values for 3 parts for a 'for' loop. If the condition is missing then the loop will become infinte.Uncomment the forOps2() method to see execution of infinite for loop.
Output:

```
Value of i :10
Value of i :9
Value of i :8
Value of i :7
Value of i :6
Value of i :5
Value of i :4
Value of i :3
Value of i :2
Value of i :1
```

We can write any legal java instructions inside any of the 3 parts of the for loop.
The next program demonstrates this behaviour.

```
//Prg2.java
//Description : Using for loop

class Program {
      static void forOps() {
              for (int i=0;i < 10 ; i++,System.out.println("In loop"))
                    System.out.println("Value of i :"+i);
      }

      public static void main(String args[]) {
              forOps();
      }
}
```

Output:

```
Value of i :0
In loop
Value of i :1
In loop
Value of i :2
In loop
Value of i :3
In loop
Value of i :4
In loop
Value of i :5
In loop
Value of i :6
In loop
Value of i :7
In loop
Value of i :8
In loop
Value of i :9
In loop
```

Summary

For loop is used mainly for fixed iterations. For loop has 3 parts i.e initialization, condition and increment.

Chapter 22
While and Do. While Loops

Topics
- ✓ **Introduction**
- ✓ **Using While loop**
- ✓ **Using Do...While loop**
- ✓ **Summary**

Introduction
In this chapter I will discuss about while and do .. while loops. Both of these loops execute as block of instructions until the condition is true, the loops are exited when the condition is false.

Using While Loop
In while loop the condition is checked before the loop is executed.The syntax of the while is as follows

Syntax :

```
while(Boolean_expression) {
        //Statements
}
```

Let's understand while loop better with help of an example.

```java
//Prg.java
//Description:Using While loop

class Program {
 static void whileOps() {
      int i=10;
      while (i > 0) {
            System.out.println("The value of i:"+i);
            i--;
      }

 }
 public static void main(String args[]) {
  whileOps();
 }
}
```

Output:

```
The value of i:10
The value of i:9
The value of i:8
The value of i:7
The value of i:6
The value of i:5
The value of i:4
The value of i:3
The value of i:2
The value of i:1
```

Using Do..While Loop

Do.. while loop is guaranteed to be executed at least once then the condition is checked.
Syntax of the do..while loop.

```
do {
        statement(s)
    } while (expression);
```

Let's understand do..while loop with help of an example.

//Prg2.java
//Description : Using Do.. While

```
class Program {
 static void dowhileOps() {
  int i=0;
  System.out.println("Do..while loop demo");
  do {
        System.out.println("The value of i:"+i);
        i++;
  } while (i<10);
 }
 public static void main(String args[]) {
  dowhileOps();
 }
}
```

Output:
```
Do..while loop demo
The value of i:0
The value of i:1
The value of i:2
The value of i:3
The value of i:4
The value of i:5
The value of i:6
The value of i:7
The value of i:8
The value of i:9
```

Summary

While loop checks the condition before execution.Do while loop execute the code block at least once and then check for condition.

Chapter 23
Break and Continue keywords

Introduction
In this chapter I will discuss about break and continue keyword. Both these keywords are used in loops such as for, while and do...while loops and break keyword is used in switch...case as well.

Using Break Keyword
It is used for exiting a loop or a case statement from a switch. The break keyword can be
a. Labelled: A means to identify area within a code block.
b. Unlabeled: No identifier associated.

Let's understand break keyword with the help of an example

```java
//Prg.java
//Description: Using break statement

class Program {
    static void breakOps() {
        int k=0;
        while (k<10) {
            if (k==5)
                break;
            k++;
        }
        System.out.println("The value of 'k' after break is:"+ k);
    }
    static void breakOps2() {
    first: // Label
        for( int i = 0; i < 3; i++) {
        second: // label
            for(int j = 0; j < 4; j ++ )
            {
                System.out.println("Value of i:"+i);
                System.out.println("Value of j:"+j);
                break first;
```

```
                    }
              }

       third: // Label
              for( int a = 0; a < 4; a++) {
                     System.out.println("The value of a:"+a);
              }

       }
       public static void main(String args[]) {
              breakOps();
              breakOps2();
       }
}
```

Output:

```
The value of 'k' after break is :5
Value of i:0
Value of j:0
The value of a:0
The value of a:1
The value of a:2
The value of a:3
```

Using Continue Keyword

The continue statement skips the current iteration of a loop. The control is return back at the starting of the loop after continue statement is executed. It can be of 2 types
   a. Labeled
   b. Unlabeled

Let's understand Continue keyword with the help of an example.

```
//Prg2.java
//Description: Using continue - labeled and unlabeled

class Program {
       static void contiOps() {
    int limit = 10;
    int facto = 1;

    OutLoop: for (int i = 1; i <= limit; i++) {
      facto = 1;
      for (int j = 2; j <= i; j++) {
        if (i > 10 && i % 2 == 1) {
          continue OutLoop;
```

```
        }
      facto *= j;
    }
    System.out.println(i + " factorial is " + facto);
  }
    }
    public static void main(String args[]) {
            contiOps();
    }
}
```

Output:
```
1 factorial is 1
2 factorial is 2
3 factorial is 6
4 factorial is 24
5 factorial is 120
6 factorial is 720
7 factorial is 5040
8 factorial is 40320
9 factorial is 362880
10 factorial is 3628800
```

Summary

Break statement is used for terminating a loop. Continue statement is used for ignoring the next set of instructions in a loop.

Chapter 24
Type Conversion and Type Casting

<u>Topics</u>
- ✓ **Introduction**
- ✓ **What is Type Conversion?**
- ✓ **What is Type Casting?**
- ✓ **Summary**

Introduction
In this chapter you will learn about type conversion and type casting. When the data that we require is not in the form that is required for further processing then data has to be converted or casted.

What is Type Conversion?
Assigning value of a variable of a type to a variable of compatible type is called as type conversion. e.g byte to int ,int to long, int to double.Type conversion does not occur between incompatible types. e.g boolean to int, int to char or a string cannot be casted to an int.
Type conversion is widening in nature i.e it occur between small type(memory) to large type(memory) e.g byte to int or int to long.

Let's understand type conversion with help of an example.

```java
//Prg.java
//Description : Working with type conversion

class Program {
        static void tcOps() { // widening (small to large)
                byte b=45;
                int i=b; // automatic conversion
                float f=b;
                double d=b;
                System.out.println("The value after conversion(byte to int) :" + i);
                System.out.println("The value after conversion(byte to double) :" + d);
        }

    public static void main(String args[]) {
        tcOps();
    }
}
```

Output:

```
The value after conversion(byte to int) :45
The value after conversion(byte to double) :45.0
```

If the conversion occur between larger type to smaller type it would yield into a compiler error.

Output:
```
Prg.java:10: error: incompatible types: possible lossy conversion from double to byte
                b=d;
                ^
1 error
```

What is Type Casting?
If destination type is smaller than source type, then it has to be explicitly casted this is called as Type Casting.

    e.g int i=10;
    byte b = (byte) I;
Let's understand type casting with help of an example.
//Prg2.java
//Description: Working with type casting

class Program {
        static void tcOps() { // Narrowing (Large to small)
                double d= 45.78979;
                float f = (float)d;
                int i = (int) d;
                long l = (long) d;
                //boolean b = (boolean) d; // compiler error
                System.out.println("The value after type casting(double to float) "+ f);
                System.out.println("The value after type casting(double to int) "+ i);
                System.out.println("The value after type casting(double to long) "+l);
        }

    public static void main(String args[]) {
        tcOps();
    }
}
Output:
```
The value after type casting(double to float) 45.78979
The value after type casting(double to int) 45
The value after type casting(double to long) 45
```

Casting cannot be done between unrelated types such as float to boolean (It will yield into compiler error).
// code

```
double d= 45.78979;
boolean b = (boolean) d; // compiler error
```

Output:

```
Prg2.java:10: error: incompatible types: double cannot be converted to boolean
            boolean b = (boolean) d; // compiler error
                        ^
1 error
```

Summary

Type conversion is automatic conversion from one to another compatible type.Type casting is explicit conversion from one to another type. Type casting cannot be done between unrelated types.

Chapter 25
Arithmetic and Relational Operators

Topics
✓ **Introduction**
✓ **What are Operators?**
✓ **Using Arithmetic Operators**
✓ **Using Relational Operators**
✓ **Summary**

Introduction
In this chapter I will discuss about how to use arithmetic and relational operators.Arithmetic and relational operators form the backbone of mathematical computation in Java.

What are Operators?
They are special symbols that perform specific operation. Operator can work with multiple operands.

Java has support for 5 types of operators
- Arithmetic
- Relational
- Bitwise
- Logical
- Assignment

Using Arithmetic Operators
They are used for creating mathematical expressions.Some of the arithmetic operators are

- \+ : Addition (Works with 2 operands)
- \- : Subtraction (Works with 2 operands)
- / : Division (Works with 2 operands)
- *: Multiplication (Works with 2 operands)
- % : Modulus (Reminder- Works with 2 operands)
- ++ : Unary Increment (Works with 1 operand)
- -- : Unary Decrement (Works with 2 operand)

Let's understand arithmetic operators with help of an example.
//Prg.java
//Description : Working with arithmetic operators

```
class Program {
    static void ariOps() {
```

```java
        int i=20,j=10;
        int sum = i+j;
        int subs = i-j;
        int prod = i*j;
        int div = i/j;
        int rem = i % j;
        i++;
        --j;
        System.out.println(" The sum is :"+ sum);
        System.out.println(" The substraction is :"+ subs);
        System.out.println(" The multiplication is :"+ prod);
        System.out.println(" The division is :"+ div);
        System.out.println(" The remainder is :"+ rem);
    }
    public static void main(String args[]) {
        ariOps();
    }
}
```

Output:

```
The sum is :30
The substraction is :10
The multiplication is :200
The division is :2
The remainder is :0
```

Using Relational Operators

Relational operators work with 2 operands.It is used for determining relationship that one operand has with another. They are used in control and looping constructs. e.g if,for,while etc. The outcome of relational expression is a boolean.
The List of relational operators is as follows

Expression	Result
op > op2	op is greater than op2
op >= op2	op is greater than or equal to op2
op < op2	op is less than to op2
op <= op2	op is less than or equal to op2
op == op2	op and op2 are equal

op != op2	op and op2 are not equal

Let's understand usage of relational operators with help of an example.

```java
//Prg2.java
//Description : Using relational expression

class Program {

    static void relOps() {
        int i=10;
        int j=20;

        if ( i == j )
            System.out.println("i is equal to j");
        if (i > j)
            System.out.println("i is greater than j");
        if (i < j)
            System.out.println("i is less than j");
        System.out.println("i==j "+(i==j));
        System.out.println("i > j "+(i>j));
        System.out.println("i < j "+(i<j));
    }

    public static void main(String args[]) {
        relOps();
    }
}
```

Output:
```
i is less than j
i==j false
i > j false
i < j true
```

Summary

Operators are special symbols that perform specific operation.The outcome of relational expression is a boolean.Arithmetic operators are used for mathematical operations.

Chapter 26
Logical and Ternary Operators

Topics
- ✓ **Introduction**
- ✓ **Using Logical Operators**
- ✓ **Using Ternary Operators**
- ✓ **Using Instanceof operator**
- ✓ **Summary**

Introduction
In this chapter I will discuss about how to use Logical, Ternary and Instanceof opertors.

Using Logical Operator
They are used for binding and checking multiple conditions together. The relational operators are bound together using logical operators. There are 4 logical operators in Java.
Logical operators in Java

Operator Symbol	Operator Name
&&	AND
||	OR
!	NOT
^	XOR

Description of logical operators.
- a. AND operator (&&) – Returns true when both the condition are true else false.
- b. OR operator(||) – Returns true when either of the condition true. It is false of both the conditions are false.
- c. NOT operator(!) – Returns true when the condition is false and is false when the condition is true.
- d. XOR operator(^) – Returns true when either of the conditions is true. It will yield false if both the conditions are true or both the conditions are false.

Let's understand logical operators with the help of examples.

```
//Prg.java
//Description: Using 'AND' operator

class Program {
  static void andOps() {
      int a=10;
```

```java
        int b=20;
        if (a > 5 && b < 25) // Is true when both conditions are true else false.
                System.out.println("Value of a,b is greater than 5 and less than 25");
        else
        {
            System.out.println("Value of a:" + a);
                System.out.println("Value of b:" + b);
        }

    }
    public static void main(String args[]) {
            andOps();
    }
}
```

Output:

Value of a,b is greater than 5 and less than 25

Let's understand usage of OR operator(||) and NOT operator(!).

```java
//Prg2.java
//Description: Using 'OR' operator

class Program {
    static void orOps() {
        int a=10;
        int b=20;
        if (a > 5 || b < 25) // Is true when either of the conditions are true else false.
                System.out.println("Value of a,b is greater than 5 and less than 25");
        else
        {
            System.out.println("Value of a:" + a);
                System.out.println("Value of b:" + b);
        }

    }
    static void notOps() {
        boolean b=true;
        if (!b)
                System.out.println("Value of b is false");
        else
        System.out.println("Value of b is true");

    }
    public static void main(String args[]) {
            orOps();
```

```
        notOps();
    }
}
```

```
Value of a,b is greater than 5 and less than 25
Value of b is true
```

Using Ternary Operator

It is used for assigning a value to a variable based on a boolean expression. It can be used as an alternative to if/else statement.

Syntax :
        result = someCondition ? value1 : value2;

        If the conditon is true then value1 is returned else value2 is returned and stored in result variable.

Let's understand ternary operator better with help of an example.

```
//Prg3.java
//Description : Using Ternary operator

class Program {
    static void terOps() {
        int j=10;
        String result = false ? "Superman is the greatest" : "Batman is better";
        System.out.println(result);
        result = j>20 ? "J is greater than 20" : "J is not less than 20";
        System.out.println(result);

    }

    public static void main(String args[]) {
        terOps();

    }
}
```

Output:
```
Batman is better
J is not less than 20
```

80

Using Instanceof Operator

It is used to check if a given variable is of a given type.It is also called as comparison operator i.e. it compares variable with type.

Let's understand instanceof operator with an example.

```
//Prg4.java
//Description : Using instanceof operator

class Program {
 static void instOps() {
        Program obj = new Program();
        if (obj instanceof Program)
                System.out.println("obj is typeof Program");
        else
                System.out.println("obj is not typeof Program");
 }
 public static void main(String args[]) {
   instOps();
 }
}
```

Output:
```
obj is typeof Program
```

If used with a null value it will return false.

```
//Prg5.java
//Description : Using instanceof operator with null

class Program {
 static void instOps() {
        Program obj=null;
        if (obj instanceof Program)
                System.out.println("obj is typeof Program");
        else
                System.out.println("obj is not typeof Program");
 }
 public static void main(String args[]) {
   instOps();
 }
}
```

Output:

obj is not typeof Program

Summary

Logical operators are used for checking multiple conditions together. Instanceof operator is used to check if a given variable of a given type.

Chapter 27
Arrays

<u>Topics</u>
- ✓ **Introduction**
- ✓ **What is an Array?**
- ✓ **Using Single Dimension Array**
- ✓ **Using Multi Dimension Array**
- ✓ **Summary**

Introduction
In this chapter you will learn about how to operate on arrays. Array is used as a storage entity for large data in memory. I will also discuss about single and multi dimension arrays.

What is an Array?
It is a data container which is used for storing data at runtime within memory. The attributes of an array are as follows
a. Fixed size – Size in bytes is known before usage.
b. Single type – It can only be of a single type.
c. Accessed using an index.
d. Index start with 0.

So the array can be defined as a container of data located in memory which of a fixed size and is of a given data type.Java arrays are safe i.e they are bounds checked. If the user accesses beyond the bounds the JVM raises an exception.

Syntax of array definition:
        Datatype arobj=new Datatype[size];

Array are used for quick and easy access to data. It eliminate the need for creating many variables. The data located in an array can be accessed using an index.

There are 2 types of arrays i.e
a. Single dimension.
b. Multi dimension.

Using Single Dimension Array
They have one row and fixed number of columns.Length property is used for getting the length of an array.

Array Declaration
- Datatype ar[];
- Datatype []ar;

Array Definition
- Datatype obj[] =new Datatype[size];
- Datatype []obj =new Datatype[size];

Let's understand usage of single dimension array with an example.

```java
//Prg.java
//Description : Working with single dimension arrays

class Program {
    static void sdOps() {
        int []ar2;
        int ar3[] = {1,2,5,6,7,8,9};
    }
    static void sdOps2() {
        int []ar = new int [5];
        ar[0]= 20;
        ar[1]=40;
        ar[2]=50;
        ar[3]=60;
        ar[4]=70;
        System.out.println("The length of the array is:"+ ar.length);
        for (int i=0;i< ar.length;i++)
            System.out.println("The location : "+ i + " has value:"+ ar[i]);
    }
    static int[] sqArray(int ar[]) {
        for (int i=0;i<ar.length;i++)
            ar[i]= ar[i]*ar[i];

        return ar;
    }
    static void show(int ar[]) {
        System.out.println("\n");
        for (int i=0;i< ar.length;i++)
            System.out.println("The location : "+ i + " has value:"+ ar[i]);
    }
    public static void main(String args[]) {
        sdOps();
        sdOps2();
        int ar[] = {1,2,5,6,7};
        int sq[] = sqArray(ar);
        show(sq);
```

```
        }
}
```

Output:

```
The length of the array is:5
The location : 0 has value:20
The location : 1 has value:40
The location : 2 has value:50
The location : 3 has value:60
The location : 4 has value:70


The location : 0 has value:1
The location : 1 has value:4
The location : 2 has value:25
The location : 3 has value:36
The location : 4 has value:49
```

If the array is accessed beyond it's bound then JVM throws an exception.
// code snapshot

```
int []ar = new int [5];
ar[0]= 20;
ar[1]=40;
ar[2]=50;
ar[3]=60;
ar[4]=70;
ar[5]=90;
```

Output:

```
Exception in thread "main" java.lang.ArrayIndexOutOfBoundsException: 5
        at Program.sdOps2(Prg.java:16)
        at Program.main(Prg.java:34)
```

Multi Dimension Array
The data is stored in combination of rows and columns.The MD array can be 2,3,4 or 'N' dimension.

MD Declaration Syntax:
- dataType[][] ar;
- dataType [][]ar;
- dataType ar[][];
- dataType []ar[];

Let's understand how to create and access 2 dimension array.

```java
//Prg2.java
//Description : Working with multidimension array

class Program {
 static void muldOps() {
  int ar[][] = {{2,3},{3,4},{6,7}};
  int []ar2[] = {{4,5},{6,7},{9,7}};
 }

 static void muldOps2() {
         int ar[][] = new int [2][2];
         ar[0][0]=5;
         ar[0][1]=1;
         ar[1][0]=3;
         ar[1][1]=7;
         for (int i=0;i< ar.length;i++) // Getting length of row
                 for (int j=0;j < ar[0].length;j++) // Getting length of column
                         System.out.println("The value at location :ar["+i+"]"+"["+j+"]"+ " is :"
+ ar[i][j]);
 }
 static int [][] muldOps3(int ar[][]) {
         ar[0][0]=ar[0][0] * ar[0][0];
         ar[0][1]=ar[0][1] * ar[0][1];
         ar[1][0]=ar[1][0] * ar[1][0];
         ar[1][1]=ar[1][1] * ar[1][1];
         return ar;
 }
 static void show(int ar[][]) {

         for (int i=0;i< ar.length;i++) // Getting length of row
                 for (int j=0;j < ar[0].length;j++) // Getting length of column
                         System.out.println("The value at location :ar["+i+"]"+"["+j+"]"+ " is :"
+ ar[i][j]);
 }


 public static void main(String args[]) {
   muldOps();
   muldOps2();

   int ar[][] = {{2,3},{3,4},{6,7}};
    System.out.println("\n Before square");
   show(ar);
```

```java
    System.out.println("\n After square");
    int ar2[][] = muldOps3(ar);
    show(ar2);


   }
}
```

Output:

```
The value at location :ar[0][0] is :5
The value at location :ar[0][1] is :1
The value at location :ar[1][0] is :3
The value at location :ar[1][1] is :7

 Before square
The value at location :ar[0][0] is :2
The value at location :ar[0][1] is :3
The value at location :ar[1][0] is :3
The value at location :ar[1][1] is :4
The value at location :ar[2][0] is :6
The value at location :ar[2][1] is :7

 After square
The value at location :ar[0][0] is :4
The value at location :ar[0][1] is :9
The value at location :ar[1][0] is :9
The value at location :ar[1][1] is :16
The value at location :ar[2][0] is :6
The value at location :ar[2][1] is :7
```

Let's understand how to create and access 3 dimension array. Length property can be used to get size of a given dimension.

        ar[0].length // Getting length of column for first row


```java
//Prg3.java
//Description : Working with multidimension array(3D)

class Program {
 static void muldOps() {
        int ar[][][] = new int [2][2][2];
        ar[0][0][0]=5;
        ar[0][0][1]=1;
        ar[0][1][0]=3;
        ar[0][1][1]=8;
```

```java
ar[1][0][0]=2;
ar[1][0][1]=9;
ar[1][1][0]=6;
ar[1][1][1]=4;

for (int i=0;i< ar.length;i++) // Getting length of row
        for (int j=0;j < ar[0].length;j++) // Getting length of column
            for (int k=0;k < ar[0][0].length;k++)
                System.out.println("The value at location
:ar["+i+"]"+"["+j+"]"+"["+k+"]"+ " is :" + ar[i][j][k]);
}


public static void main(String args[]) {
  muldOps();
}
}
```

Output:
```
The value at location :ar[0][0][0] is :5
The value at location :ar[0][0][1] is :1
The value at location :ar[0][1][0] is :3
The value at location :ar[0][1][1] is :8
The value at location :ar[1][0][0] is :2
The value at location :ar[1][0][1] is :9
The value at location :ar[1][1][0] is :6
The value at location :ar[1][1][1] is :4
```

Summary

Array is container of data in memory. It is of fixed size and is of a given data type. Length property return the size of the current dimension.

Chapter 28
Jagged Arrays

Topics
- ✓ **Introduction**
- ✓ **Using Jagged Array**
- ✓ **Summary**

Introduction
In this chapter I will discuss about how to create and use Jagged array. Jagged array helps in better utilization of memory by allow to create arrays which fit user's need.

Using Jagged Array
It is a multi dimension array in which the columns can vary for each row. The rows are identified first then the columns are identified for each row.This helps in allocation of memory as per requirement which saves memory wastage.

Syntax:

```
int ar[][] = new int[2][];
ar[0] = new int[2];   // The first row will have 2 columns
ar[1] = new int[3];  // The second row will have 3 columns
```

Let's understand jagged arrays with help of an example.

```
//Prg.java
//Description : Working with jagged arrays

class Program {
    static void jaggOps() {
        int ar[][] = new int[3][];
        ar[0]=new int [1];
        ar[1] = new int[2];
        ar[2] = new int [3];
        for(int i=0;i<ar.length;i++)
            for(int j=0;j<ar[i].length;j++)
                ar[i][j] = i*j;

        for(int i=0;i<ar.length;i++)
            for(int j=0;j<ar[i].length;j++)
                System.out.println("The value at location :ar["+i+"]"+"["+j+"]"+ " is :" + ar[i][j]);
```

```
    }
    public static void main(String args[]) {
        jaggOps();
    }

}
```

```
The value at location :ar[0][0] is :0
The value at location :ar[1][0] is :0
The value at location :ar[1][1] is :1
The value at location :ar[2][0] is :0
The value at location :ar[2][1] is :2
The value at location :ar[2][2] is :4
```

The numbers rows are 2. For 1st row there are 2 columns and the second row has 3 columns.

Summary
In Jagged array the number of columns can vary.Jagged array help in optimizing memory usage.

Chapter 29
For Each Loop

Topics
- ✓ **Introduction**
- ✓ **Using For Each Loop**
- ✓ **Summary**

Introduction
In this chapter we will discuss about how to iterate over arrays using For Each loop. It better and simplier to use for each loop over other loops for aggregates.

Using For Each Loop
This was introduced in Java 5. For each loop is used for iterating over arrays and collections i.e it is a loop that is exclusively to used for against aggregates. For each loop is less error prone compared to for,while and do..while loops because there is no condition check involved hence is simplier and safer to use.

Salient features
- a. No increment required
- b. No Condition check required

Syntax :
        for(data_type variable : array | collection)   { }

Let's understand the usage of for each loop with help of an example.
Using for each with single dimension array.
//Prg.java
//Description : for.. each loop with single dimension array

```
class Program {
      static void foreachOps() {
            int ar[] = {1,2,3,4,5,6,7};
            for(int i : ar)
               System.out.print(i+" ");

      }

      public static void main(String args[]) {
            foreachOps();
      }
}
```

Output:
```
1 2 3 4 5 6 7
```

The for each loop can also be used with multi dimension array. The outer loop iterate over rows and inner loop over columns.

//Prg2.java
//Description : for.. each loop using with multi dimension array

```java
class Program {

        static void foreachOps() {
                int ar[][] = {{13,22},{36,43},{56,68},{71,83}};
                for(int i[] : ar)
                        for (int j : i)
                                System.out.print(j+" ");
        }
        public static void main(String args[]) {
                foreachOps();
        }
}
```

Output:
```
13 22 36 43 56 68 71 83
```

Summary

For each was introduced in Java 5. Foreach loop is used for iterating over arrays and collections.